Sucking SUG

(Dreams in

Barbara Griffith-Bourne

Sunesis Ministries Ltd

Sucking Sugar Cane (Dreams in Paradise)

Published by Sunesis Ministries Ltd. For more information about Sunesis Ministries Ltd, please visit:

www.stuartpattico.com

ISBN: 978-0-9956837-0-9

CONTENTS

◊

◊

WHY I WAS COMPELLED TO WRITE THIS BOOK

This came about as an idea from my Niece, Jemmelle. One day, her father and another brother and I were reminiscing with amusement about the experiences of our childhood when Jemmelle exclaimed, "Why don't you all write a book called, "Sucking Sugar-cane" – suggesting that she would write the book if we provided the material?

Ooop! Sorry Jem, I've jumped the gun and went ahead of you; please forgive me, should this Book falls below your excellent standard – I'm looking for at least a 'B'- Plus?

Umm; umm .... grovel; grovel; could you please write the 'Foreword'?

'Sucking Sugar Cane' – Foreword by Jemmelle Griffith

◊

Bajan Proverb: *'Force ripe fruit don' got nuh taste'* (This is used metaphorically to show disapproval of clever behaviour in children).

I started this foreword with the proverb, as I am sure when you start *'Sucking Sugar Cane'*, many old proverbs will come to call.

'Sucking Sugar Cane' is akin to taking a ride in a Caribbean tardis travelling up and down the island, back in time and up to the present. This touches all your senses, from smelling waves break up in Bathsheba, tasting cuckoo and okra at your uncle's house or feeling the breeze on your face whilst on a ZR going 'town'.

I am very fortunate to be part of a family where telling 'tales' and family folklore is essential and extremely common place. The author Barbara 'Ruby' Griffith-Bourne is my paternal aunt. We are a passionately vocal and expressive family – I am so pleased that Ruby has decided to capture and record these thoughts, feelings and experiences in this book. All too often these stories are only written in the 'air' and not written down for the generations yet to come. To maintain their potency, they need to be savoured and cherished.

I have always been proud to be Bajan and I love the uniqueness of our culture; the singsong nature of our voices, the emphasis when relaying even the simplest information, and the exaggerated drawl when we say things like "maaaan, I would tek muh Collins and cut 'e"!

Being British born Bajan, I have been fortunate enough to go 'back home' and experience the island first hand. When reading Chapter 22 'Bajan Crop Over', it took me straight back to my first visit almost 16 years ago (time duhs fly yeh?!), as well as my Dad recalling how he wasn't allowed to attend 'Kadooment' so would watch it on the TV and "pelt my wais" and wring up me shirt"!

This is what you get when 'Sucking Sugar Cane'; and opportunity to be mentally and emotionally transported 'back' home'.

I hope you enjoy and feel 'sweet fuh days'!

Jemmelle Griffith

Niece and Poet

Author of: 'I always knew I was a Goddess'

Lower Sydenham, London, UK

ABOUT THE AUTHOR

~~~**~~~

Born to parents from Barbados, Poet and Author, Barbara Griffith-Bourne was partly raised by her grandmother, a couture Seamstress and Evangelist who help influence her passion for poetry by encouraging her and other members of the family to read portions from the Bible and classical literature, before bedtime.

Partly educated in Barbados, Barbara later emigrated to the United Kingdom to join her mother, where she continued and finished her education. When Barbara became a Christian, she prayed to receive the gift to write poetical lyric. This inspirational gift came as a result of a testing life's experience which, at times for Barbara was very traumatic. But because God, the Father is faithful, **her desire has been truly realised for His purpose** - to be of great inspirational help to others!

Although Barbara enjoys writing poetry, her focus is on the **'spoken word'** for which she has, for over ten years undertaken many **'Poetic Recitals'** at various events nationally and internationally, which brought much inspiration, pleasure and refreshment to people in diverse audiences.

~**~

ACKNOWLEDGEMENTS

◊

I extend my grateful thanks and appreciation to all those who supported and encouraged me. I'm grateful also for their input in enabling me to write this book.

Forgive duh 'Bajan dialect' but, 'Nuff thanks' to muh family members, friends and relatives who gave me encouragement, support, tips and ideas - (You know who you are!).

 Yet, I must give a mention to Hartley, my brother who urged me on and greatly encouraged me, checking time after time with me to see how far I've progressed and reminding me of events in our past – Nuff Love, Bro.

Special thanks to Brother Elvin, whose constant invaluable support I could not do without; from the beginning providing needed backing for my poetic venture; yet while teasing me ..... "wuh's dat yuh writing a tall, a tall ...?" 'D', I know yuh proud a muh, but yuh doh want muh to know. Much Love and Respect, Bro.

Elaine, my Sister, who took the time to read the manuscript when it was in its infancy and her husband, Andrew who offered invaluable suggestions – Love and Blessings to you both!

Wendy, my daughter, who willingly helped with editing the manuscript and offered helpful suggestions – Love and Blessings!

Special thanks to daughter, Marisa and her son, Lukas who helped with new technology issues, without which I couldn't complete this book. Love and Blessing to you both!

Special thanks to Jemmelle, my niece, who willing supported me and offered invaluable suggestions. Furthermore, I am grateful to her for the "Foreword" which she wrote! - (Lotta Love, girl; I owe yuh one)!

Special mention and thanks to the late Dave Kensley Maloney whose contribution was invaluable. Rest in Peace, Bro.

Most of all, I assign 'Maximum Respect' to my best friend, 'Jeshua' (otherwise known as 'Jesus -The Saviour of the World') who constantly inspired me with joyous enthusiasm and wisdom thus, making it easy to write this book - I LOVE YOU FOREVER!

◊

INTRODUCTION

CROP-TIME AND SUGAR-CANE – A VENTURE OF WHICH
BARBADOS WAS FAMED!

◊

In a quest to re-capture some of my childhood experiences and treasured times I spent in the land of my nativity, I find myself reminiscing time and time again when my spirit takes a leap to the Caribbean!

◊

'Sucking Sugar Cane' (Dreams in Paradise), is a story of my primary years living in Barbados and as an adult when I revisited the Island with my family and relatives.

As I paint the picture of my adventurous experience, please feel free to catch the vision in essence. Should you desire to take the journey, you may find the ride bumpy or smooth, so fasten your seat belts as you choose!

13

Again, in reading this story, it may seem bitter-sweet, yet, I urge you to look on it as a treat. Please feel free also to laugh-out-loud at the humour and comical quotes, don't bother to leave any $10dollar notes – yuh still can if yuh want tuh – duh sey every little helps!!

I want you not to point the finger at anyone nor to apportion blame, neither say, "What a shame"! This story gave me great excitement when it I compiled and, it's no word of a lie!

◊

I've chosen to relate this story in poetic genre to hopefully, tickle your taste buds and **spice up** your enjoyment as you read.

I've thrown in some 'Bajan Lingo' too, sporadically, throughout the text and have provided some interpretation appropriately. The 'Lingo' might jog the memory of older folk; perhaps, even dat of the younger generation, their vocabulary to provoke!

Sucking sweet sugar-cane
Is a pleasure that's still the same!
What an enjoyable delight?
When sitting out in the moonlight

On a clear starry night;
Telling stories and cracking jokes
Of days gone by and customs of old folks!
Excuse me now, as I rhapsodize -
As thrills of my past with the present collides!
My dreams, I'll heroically recapture,
By aspiration and factual adventure!
❖ ◇ ❖
◊

CHAPTER 1
◊

BIRTH PLACE DREAM
❖✦❖

Come dream with me of my birthplace -
A land of my heritage and race;
Blessed place of my nativity
That holds treasured memories for me!
❖✦❖
It boasts the most breathtaking views,
An island where the sun-seeker pursues;
Where a fusion of 'Steel Band music,
Engages the heart in a melodious grip!
❖✦❖
Priding 'Cuckoo' as its national dish,
Topped by mouth-watering flying fish!
'Land of Paradise' is its ethos;
You guessed; sundrenched Barbados!
❖✦❖
◊

CHAPTER 2

◊

CROP-TIME

❖◇❖

The highlight of the year was crop-time

When, we sucked 'Sugar-cane' oh so fine;
Out in the beauty of the moonlight,
Till the clocks struck midnight!
See the little ones suck and grin
Until the juice flow down their chin!
There were different types of cane
Which we all knew by name
But, the soft 'Brown-skin Girl'
Was to us the sweetest in the world!
We'd chew up even cane knot -
So delicious, we'd not want to stop!

❖✧❖

Groups of Labourers worked with joy
As lively chatter their mouth employ;
Men and women were part of the crew
Some wearing no boot or shoe!

❖✧❖

Hundreds worked in the cane field,
Cutting and bundling the yield!
Families would in harvesting engage
To maximise their living wage;
Some small children aged nine
Worked without receiving a dime!

❖✧❖

Men loaded the cane on Lorries

For transport to the sugar factories!
Could've been 'Swans' or 'Bruce Vale' -
One, where there's profit and sale!

❖◇❖

Again, I distinctly call to mind
In the season of crop-time
Seeing young boys running a muck
Hopping on and off a loaded cane truck;
Supposedly to steal a free ride,
Alas; some ended up on 'the other side'!
Sad to say, a lesson some did not learn –
Believing only, they must have their turn?

❖◇❖

◊

CHAPTER 3

◊

DREAMS & REALITY

❖✧❖

❖✧❖

I often dream of the idyllic **'East Coast'**

Where I dearly loved to be most;

To inhale the fresh sea air I crave

Watching the breaking of the dashing waves!
There, the sweetest breeze in motion
Sweeps across from the Atlantic Ocean!
❖◇❖
Being there, lying on the coral sands
Clutching treasured shells in my hands!
Excitedly sharing my siblings humour –
Bursting into fits of joyful laughter;
Appreciating God's wonderful creation,
Giving Him thanks with adoration!
(The therapeutic splashing of the wave
Adheres to the commandment God gave)!
❖◇❖
Unforgettable is tranquil **'Back River'** -
I recall countless childhood adventure;
Romping and playing hide and seek;
Somewhat, making this nostalgia complete!
❖◇❖
Picking native fruits, hunting crayfish,
Throwing pebbles in the water, making a wish!
Sitting on the river bank in calm repose -
The desired spot while eating mangoes!
❖◇❖
Memories of eating juicy wine-berry
With fearless cousin, Orrie;
Who climbed to the tree-top

Shaking the branch for the fruit to drop!

Taking in the scenic views at night
Is by all means a delightsome sight
Especially graced by brilliant moonlight!
Hearing the water beat against the rocks,
In even motion like time-clocks!
Sitting amongst the sandy wild vine,
Under the shiny stars by design!
Why does conversation a tribute pay
To an era of a by-gone day?

❖ ◇ ❖
◊

'Jarrett Pasture' - our treasured playground
Where, with like-minds our fun was found;
Anyone for a game of 'Rounders', now?
We played that game for hours, somehow!
Yet, at times we had to retreat
When victory was ours, though not defeat!

❖ ◇ ❖

Cricket loved de Cricket -
At 'Jarrett pasture', I saw it;
Potential, similar to Everton Weeks -
Young boys their cricketing careers seek;
Showing expertise at the 'Crease'

24

When a fast-bowler his ball released!

(Not Jarrett)

'Jarrett Pasture' has a lot to answer for -
A magnet for fun and bad behaviour!
My cousin and I were always up to tricks
Despite the fact we got plenty licks;
Being between aged seven to ten,
Perhaps, it didn't matter to us then?
We didn't disobey purposely, I must add

As our actions made us so sad!
Being young we were generally daring;
Innocence playing a part without misgiving!
❖◈❖
We went right ahead and did our thing;
Overstaying at play on the dodgy swing!
We couldn't hide our bruises with a plot –
The tell-tale sign was our torn frock!
❖◈❖
Too afraid to go home one day,
Not knowing what our parents might say;
We decided to sleep-out near our house,
Trying hard to keep as still as a mouse!
But as night fell and it grew dark,
I thought, 'cousin and I would have to part;
(I'm the one who gets easily frighten)
I better to go home and get beaten
Or, I'll get cuddled and be forgiven'?
I relented and crept home like a wet puppy
For I was too scared of de 'Duppy'!
Please don't ask about the outcome –
Well... someone got a very sore bottom!
❖◈❖
◊

CHAPTER 4

◊

COUNTRY BUCK

❖ ◇ ❖

❖ ◇ ❖
What a ting is dis?
I didn't know dis name exist
Until I was called, yuh 'Country Buck'
Or, 'you from duh goat-hill', names as such!
Bajans just like giving others nick-names;
Being a tease and playing funny games!
❖ ◇ ❖
Living in the idyllic country

Was not all about being healthy;
More like being at one with nature,
Learning lessons from each living creature!
❖ ❖ ❖
At midnight, hearing the dogs barking,
Being woken by the cock crowing;
Kept awake by cats meowing;
The woeful cooing of doves at dusk
And other wild life was a must!
❖ ❖ ❖
Living on a farm didn't help the noise -
Our ears were intermittently poised;
The galloping of the proud turkeys,
Quacking of ducks when they see monkeys;
The contention of the farm fowls,
The hooting of the occasional owls!
❖ ❖ ❖
We naturally adapted to most chores
Assisting in pairs of two's or four's;
Tending the stubborn goats and sheep,
Aiding with 'Sorrel' harvest reap -
(Dried and use at Christmas time)
As our treat of sweet exotic wine!
❖ ❖ ❖
Some chores were most enjoyable
Like, tending my small animal -

A tender goat named, Ruby
Who sweetly skipped upon the Lea;
My touch and voice it would aptly heed
When I guided it the place to feed
But, joys inevitably come to an end -
As these goats were raised for the oven!
❖ ◆ ❖
Living in the country, we had to be content
With self-made home entertainment!
Most people had access to 'Rediffusion'
Where it was possible for a connection!
Not many households had a TV;
That would have been a luxury!
❖ ◆ ❖
Uncle had provided us a 'Grundig' radio
With international frequencies on the go;
I never got tired of hearing Pat Boone's
'Beyond the Sunset', a sweet becoming tune!
Bobby Darren was my other favourite;
Bellowing out his enticing music!
❖ ◆ ❖
At times we had a 'family talent evening' –
Everyone playing a part with thanksgiving!
Pappy and Richard played the 'Mouth-organ' –
(An instrument now seemed forgotten)!
❖ ◆ ❖

I loved when Mum read story books
With such conviction, your emotion shook!
Stories mainly about International Twins;
Their home and what they encountered therein!
These tales held us clearly spellbound;
We didn't move to spend a penny or pound!
Authored by Lucy Fitch Perkins,
Written specially for young children!
❖◇❖
These were some I could remember;
"The Colonial Twins of Virginia";
"The Twins of the American Revolution";
Those of 1812 and others from Belgian!
I'm sure there were "The Mexican Twins";
"The Swiss and Spartan Twins"!
I can't rack muh brain much more;
Don't want to leave it feeling sore!
❖◇❖
This incident I well remember though -
It being donkey years ago;
The day I wore my favourite red dress
With a sash, trimmings and the rest ...?
❖◇❖
I followed my brothers our cows to water
Where they were at verdant 'Back River';

One cow spotted my red dress
And targeted me for its conquest!
I took off as fast as my feet could carry me
Safely escaping up a tall shady tree!
You could hear my loud screams for help
While my racing heart-beat I fearfully felt!
❖◇❖
That stupid cow steered at me wagging its head,
Intimidating me instead of being fed;
My siblings all had a belly of laughs ...
I think now that the cow was with calf
Perhaps, causing it to fret
But, it was soon removed, to its regret!

❖◇❖
◊

Some things I must call to mind –
Are antiques that Bajan folk may've left behind;
Anyone remember duh 'flour bag'
Re-invented as tea towels or dish rags?
These were used to make all types of attire,
Shirts, dresses and anything one desire!
Also, people added coloured ink
Of which some dresses were dyed pink!
❖◇❖
Yuh remember duh 'Scrid-mat' -

The 'crocus-bag' on which you sat;
Suitably comfortable and soft
Crocheted with bits of multi-coloured cloth?
❖◇❖
What bout duh 'Calabash' bowl
Used for soup or whatever it would hold?
Part of utensils were these
Owned by individuals or large families!
❖◇❖
What bout duh 'Tinning Tots'
Useful as Crayfish pots
Set on rocks or clay brick
When you'd go on fishing trips?
These 'Tots' derived from milk tins
Used as cups to put yuh cocoa-tea in!
❖◇❖
We used tots as a telephone invention,
Attached to them was a wire connection;
These really work as a matter of fact,
If only around the neighbourhood for contact!
❖◇❖
Some had things suave, you bet –
The best China-ware and the etiquette;
We'd not show-off or the antiques despise –
They're part of our heritage, so we'll not them criticise!
❖◇❖

CHAPTER 5

FEEDING TIME

❖ ◆ ❖

Do Bajans still call every hot drink Tea?
Mercy me! "Susan where's muh choc-lit tee"?
Growing up, we got 'Coffee-tea' in the morning
Or 'Chocolate-tea' and boil dumpling!

❖ ◆ ❖

At night it was 'Cocoa-tee', if it befits;
'Milo-tea' or creamy 'Horlicks!
I hope Bajans distinguish them now?
It is enough to confuse duh poor cow!

❖ ◆ ❖

Good we were fed three meals a day –
That was our dear 'Mammy's' way;
Corn meal porridge, cheese and Biscuit;
Choc-lit Tea with dumplings in it!

❖ ◆ ❖

Lunch time was Okra-laden 'Cuckoo
Topped with salt-fish gravy too!
Typical ground food suitably complete
With beef, poultry or sheep-belly meat!

❖ ◆ ❖

Evening meal was Rice and Peas

Yet, someone in the family rejected these!
Hefty meals were mainly in 'Crop-time'
Or when 'Pappy' engage workers by design!
❖◇❖
Mammy loved to give us a surprise –
Something to feast our belly and eyes;
Sugary 'Cassava-bread' with 'Rice and milk',
With creamy coconut smooth as silk!
❖◇❖
At times it would be smoked salt-fish
With stewed sweet potato, as we wished!
These were home grown and freshly dug,
Free from pesticides or bug!
❖◇❖
In 'hard times' we sold fruits from our Orchard;
Scarce though, were Apples call 'Custard'!
Plentiful were Fat-pork, and Cashews –
Most people preferring these by two's!
❖◇❖
Ok! I won't forget 'Bakes' and 'Cornmeal Pap';
Not like fancy Mac Muffin or Wrap;
Cooking was done in the open-fire, wide,
Yet, we had an oil-stove besides!
❖◇❖
Our Mammy was a proficient Dressmaker,
Evangelist and Fashion Designer!

Plenty bridal gowns she sew
And attire for male and female, not a few!
❖❖❖
We helped thread the 'Singer' sewing machine
And appropriate objects to her did bring!
She had the right to be asking
For she was frequently multi-tasking!
❖❖❖
A **'do-gooder'**, she helped one and all;
Like a physician, she was always on call!
To us, her life was cut too short
When, her duty death did abort?
❖❖❖
Our home I deem a 'Walton' scenario -
A unique story and a top family show,
With mishaps and real-life adventures
Wrapped-up in mysterious treasures!
❖❖❖
◊

CHAPTER 6

◊

FONDNESS OF 'CHRIST CHURCH'

❖ ◇ ❖

I loved being with my paternal granny,
Who lived in Sergeant's Village Tenantry;
Playing fun games with a cherished cousin;
Picking 'Dunks' in the holiday season!

❖ ◇ ❖

Granny worked at 'Durants Plantation',
Weeding grass in straight motion!
She would take cousin 'M' and I along;
Our feet braving the scorching ground!
Granny shaded us with a banana leaf
From the blazing sun in chief!

❖ ◇ ❖

Christ Church was my great delight;
Visiting the 'Drive-in' shows at night;
A far cry from remote Cheltenham
Where darkness spoilt your well-paid plan!

❖ ◇ ❖

The **'Drive-in'** was close to Granny's place;
Viewing romantic movies for me was ace!
It was eye-opening although I was a child
But movies in that era were suitably mild?

❖ ◇ ❖

Dear Aunt Gwen lived nearby;
She dried many a tear from my weeping eye;
I was blessed to have her as an 'Auntie',
To mentor and inspire me!
She was called a woman of prayer,
Who relied on its mighty power each day!
From my birth she was part of my life
Especially during my childhood's strife!
Her care and loving affection
Helped steer me in the right direction!
We spent many happy hours together,
Of immense fun and laughter!
She was kind, but yet firm –
Hugs and kisses I didn't have to earn!
❖✧❖
Like friends we'd engage in conversation
When I would to her, pose many a question;
To answer me she'd not deem it a task,
Despite numerous ones I would ask!
❖✧❖
My cousins and I would share her bed
When we visited the old homestead;
We jostled for a place on her lap,
Where often very young I sat!
❖✧❖

She was not well-off but gave us 'Riches' -
A wealth of Love and Kisses!
Money cannot buy this type of treasure
Which she gave us without measure!

❖✧❖
◊

❖✧❖
◊

Revisiting Christ Church is still fond for me
As there's a welcome from Brother, Dave and family;
Tons of laughter, fun and games

Complemented by Cuckoo from his wife, Elaine!

❖ ❖ ❖

A joy too to see Brother, Richard and other relatives;

Reminiscing of how we used to live;

Some memories bitter; some sweet,

But I deem it all treasures I'd keep;

Giving thanks always is good

As it helps strengthen the brotherhood!

❖ ❖ ❖

◊

CHAPTER 7
◊

HERBAL REMEDIES
❖◆❖
When through the woods we'd trek
I'm often the target for a bet;
This important test to my memory
Would my siblings pose to name the trees?
Indigenous plants and porous shrubs,
Healing herbs and strange bulbs!
❖◆❖
Senior folk knew a lot bout **'Bush-tea'**;
Especially, bitter 'Surcee'
Used mainly to ward off duh Flu
And 'Wonder-world' leaf for cures too!
Should one child cough a little, or more
Everyone gets 'Bush-tea' for sure;
Mammy says, "Prevention is better than cure"!
❖◆❖
Never mind whether yuh bowels had duh urge,
We had to line up for duh usual purge!
No point tinking duh purge you'll escape,
You either drink it or you'd miss yuh bakes!

(Eh, ... young ones, I mean 'Laxative',
So don't be puzzled, just forgive!)
❖◆❖
Senior folks knew a lot bout 'Licks' –
On yuh back or anywhere they pick;
Please don't go pass when this happen,
You too would get a whack on yuh bottom!
If yuh make faces or tease yuh sibling,
You'd be in for another whacking!
❖◆❖
Running to the Doctor was not a novelty
When living in the heart of the country;
Folks resorted to 'tried and tested' remedies
To cure sickness and pain to ease!
❖◆❖
Pleasantly tasting herbal teas
Were given to new mothers and babies;
'Fit-weed', 'Garden Balsam' and 'White Sage'
Were among others their appetites engaged!
❖◆❖
Several antidotes were used for headache;
External and internal to take!
Your head was bandaged with 'Castor oil leaves'
Or a splash of 'Bay Rum' making yuh sneeze!
You may get a spoonful of 'Falernum' –
Ooops! For this I owe Mammy a confession!

For chesty colds, people use 'Termagine'
Or 'Camphorated oil' with its fragrant zing!
Common 'pot salt' acted to prevent Tetanus
If you stepped on a nail with rust;
'Iodex' was applied to mysterious boils
And covered so yuh clothes didn't get soiled!

❖◇❖

Anyone heard bout duh 'Watson-kernal'?
Dis one sure got me baffled!
If for it yuh wanted a cure
Yuh had to 'pee on a hot rock', fuh sure!
Listen! This is what I was told
Dat duh cure is hundreds of years old!

❖◇❖

Good old 'Candle grease';
It never disappoint in bringing relief!
If yuh had a splinter in yuh toe
This brings it out in a day or so!
Mind you, we had 'Phensic' on the shelf
And other prescribed tonics for health!

❖◇❖

Now, dis is muh brother's story –
The logic of which is hard to see;
He, when a child; poor fella
Had an attack of duh 'Eggya' -

(A severe type of troublesome fever
From which it was hard to recover!)
Doctor prescribed him yellow 'Ju-cies',
And he drank two case-full of dese!
Could it be he and duh Doctor was in cahoots?
What was wrong with 'Fresh fruit'?
❖ ❖ ❖
I'd say he was given a rare treat;
Only ting, he still skinning he teet! (Laughing)
No prizes for any correct guessing;
This is one of me crafty siblings,
Duh one who got a bowl-full of dumplings
When duh fowl-cock tek meat from he plate
As woeful cries he pretended to make?
❖ ❖ ❖
You may easily guess who this is?
For his cunning acts he should be in show-biz;
I don't tink I should give yuh a clue;
He might wanna pay me back too?
Subtle art is his cunning tricks
Yet beautifully carved are his walking sticks!
His unique paintings - sublime pictures;
His couture skill he masters;
He appears to have the 'Midas touch' -
In a class of his own, as such!

CHAPTER 8

◊

DADDY'S LITTLE GIRL

❖◇❖

Dreams of my late father often stood
In recalling happy times of my childhood;
Being 'Daddy's little girl' back then
Until he was ushered to sweet Heaven!

❖◇❖

She knew she was 'daddy's little girl'
And for her, daddy was her world!
Wherever he was, she wanted to be,
Although this was an impossibility!

❖◇❖

While at home around the farm
She would run into daddy's strong arms
As some animals made her afraid;
At times, she became very scared!

❖◇❖

Whenever daddy went away
She would often kneel and pray
Believing that Daddy God was near
Who would dry her falling tear!

❖◇❖

At times she would sob and weep
Until she cried herself to sleep;

Looking forward to daddy's home-coming
Anticipating gifts he would be bringing!
❖✦❖
Her junior years, especially
Were cherished times of quality;
She and daddy would make and fly kites;
Also, strolling 'Bridgetown' some nights!
❖✦❖
Circumstances caused her to go abroad -
Sad separation bears no sweet reward;
Although she and daddy were miles apart,
She was still 'daddy's girl' in her heart!
❖✦❖
Through ill-health daddy went to the USA
For a rest and a long holiday;
He'd plan to meet his little girl on that day
But the 'plane had a severe delay!
❖✦❖
As daddy's plane flew out, hers flew in;
On the tarmac it was landing,
So by minutes she missed him –
Never to see him alive again
As death took him, all the same!
❖✦❖
Her later years seem mournfully lean,
As Daddy's sudden death was like a dream?

Longing for his presence and touch,
To hear his sweet voice she loved so much!
❖◇❖
Would I forever long for Daddy?
Even in adulthood and over forty?
Daddy's restless Spirit thought this wrong,
My crying for him had gone on too long!
❖◇❖
I dreamt that he was quite upset
That I carried on crying for him, yet;
I was just about to rush into his arms
When, abruptly he stopped me; to my alarm
Saying, "Don't touch me and stop crying" -
Telling me that his spirit is still living!
This prompted me, with my life to move on
And accept that, from this life daddy's one!
◊
❖◇❖

CHAPTER 9

◊

<u>SUNDAY BEST</u>

❖◇❖

Religion played a part in most families' lives;
Church on Sunday seemed heavenly wise!
At primary school we went to the village church,
A quaint white building whereon birds perched;
A restful haven and landmark
Where village people's faith did start!

❖◇❖

Teachers took pupils there mid-week
Where, solace in songs they did seek;
Lead by the Head Teacher at will
The school would visit the little chapel!
❖◇❖
Once, the Priest let me off the hook,
When I put sticky toffee in his 'Prayer Book';
"Father, Father, the book got dirty" –
Was my lame excuse and pity
To the kindness he'd shown
As I didn't have a book of my own!
A lesson I did quickly learn
That, other privileges I must earn!
Sadly, the church was left in disrepair
Until it was demolished, anyway!
❖◇❖
My cherished occasion was aged 9 -
A joyous and hopeful time!
Practising for the Harvest festival;
Wearing a new dress and giving a recital!
There was nothing so captivating
As hearing melodious voices singing -
"Bringing in the Sheaves",
While children wave their Palm leaves!
❖◇❖

Seeing the produce of plentiful crops –
Sugar cane; Bananas and Sour-sops;
Plantain; golden ears of Corn,
Freshly plucked – newly born!
Water coconuts; Yams and Mangoes;
Golden Apples, Pumpkin and sweet Potatoes!
❖✧❖
Cabbage; Okra and Christaphine;
All or many things, green;
Laid out on tables and the floor;
Hanging from the ceiling and much more!
The Church was decorated with such zest
As Farmers and others gave their best!
❖✧❖
◊

CHAPTER 10

◊

OLD-FASHION CHRISTMAS
❖◇❖

Oh..., the smell of fruit-filled cake
And other delicacies Mammy would bake!
Yes! **'Sweet-bread'**, **'Pudding'** and **'Pone'**,
The enticing sweets of a Bajan home!
❖◇❖
The air being filled with bakery smell
Enough to make yuh belly swell?
Children happily playing together
Outdoors in the cool sunny weather;
Anticipating their portion of sweets
Which they couldn't wait to eat!
❖◇❖
Leg of Ham was a savoury treat;
Pork, Turkey and other types of meat!
Good old Sorrel was the national drink
Was there need for alcohol? - Just think!
❖◇❖
Villagers mostly went to midnight Mass -
Should they stay-up 'til the hour's past?
The Nativity play was another thing –
Expectations of activity it would bring!
❖◇❖

Who would play the special parts?
Touting for business like in Broadway Arts;
"Please, please, I must be Mary,
I'm good at playing her – me, me"!
No, no, - I never got to be Mary,
But tried to accept whatever would be?
I was picked to be an Angel or a Star;
At times, a Shepherd coming from afar!
❖ ◆ ❖
Parents were proud of their offspring
Whether they did act or sing!
Presents for us were out of the question;
We were mostly happy with the celebration!
Yet, we dearly loved Christmas –
Being told that gifts were for Jesus!
❖ ◆ ❖
Yet, we still got some toys
That Daddy bought for us girls and boys;
One sibling got a red double-decker bus
With automatic engine as a plus!
Brother 'R' got a rock-engine truck
Which, to the floor it often got stuck!
My toy was a yellow 'warbler bird'
But someone got the 'blue' one I'd preferred!
❖ ◆ ❖

Brother 'D' got a tractor and trailer;
That would bump into the furniture!
Its exact colour I can't remember;
But this I can surely call to mind –
The squabbles over the toys at times
Which, attracted some parental discipline
And a few smacks for certain!
❖◇❖
Talk 'bout brought up strict, 'fuh-so';
We weren't allowed to sing 'Calypso',
Neither secular songs like pop –
Told; these are 'gumba' so yuh better not!
❖◇❖
Guess who got a hard smack?
Someone said I was caught in the act!
One 'tell-tale Topsy' said I didn't comply
But, I assure you, it was a big fat lie!
"Where is my wondering boy tonight",
Was the song I was singing and, that's right!
Most times you'd live on tender-hooks
As you dare not give anyone a funny look!
❖◇❖
◊

CHAPTER 11

◊

RE-VISITING EXPERIENCES AND ADVENTURE
❖ ◆ ❖

A past experience is like a dream
Or, a mysterious play it may seem;
Prompting me to ask –
"Was it a tale with Actors cast"?
Then, I remember there's a vivid scar
Which dispel myths and doubts mar!

❖ ◆ ❖

❖ ◆ ❖

It's always a joy to go back again and again;

'Although plane fares are costly, in the main;
Visiting **St Simons** is always a must
To check out some land marks is a plus!

❖◇❖

The pilgrimage to our family's house spot,
Bears marks of a land time forgot;
On the way travelling we would see
Derelict farms and wrecked cane factories;
Sights of rusting abandoned vehicles;
Makes somewhat, an awful spectacle!
Not often would we see anyone around -
It appears a foreboding ghost town!

❖◇❖

Revisiting there - times I can't reckon;
As if my childhood era still beckons;
Bearing an air of excitement
Where the past meets with the present;
Looking up an old friend;
Hearing echoes of conversations back then!
The population has seriously decreased,
Causing an absence of man and beast!

❖◇❖

Along the path to our ancestral land
Is the quaint village of Cheltenham;
Bearing the marks of a by-gone age

Yet, we could its connection engage -
Rehearsing a verse from a historical page;
Expressing it in vivid detail,
Not omitting inch or nail!
A place where our spirit and heart unite
In joyous laughter as when we flew kites
Or fetching water from the stand pipe!
In an effort to seek childhood thrills,
We'd head for the **'Ridge'**, a desire to fulfil;
I would run to conquer the hills as proof
Trying hard to re-capture my youth!

❖ ◈ ❖

◊

A few times I visited **Harrison's cave;**
Going underground I thought myself brave!
We entered by means of a 'Tramway'
And hard hats we had to wear;
Like entering a densely crystal kingdom -
A setting of a unique phenomenon;
Droplets of crystallized limestone,
Through the partial light is shown;
It has its own rare beauty,

Unmatched by anything on land or sea!
❖✧❖
I was filled with a sense of awe –
It was the most glorious 'live Art' I saw!
We walked by a waterfall of wonder;
Some say, "It's a work of nature"
Bearing the hallmark of 'The **Creator**'"!
Verbally, could anyone its beauty justify?
Sight is the source on which to rely!
It is absolutely a "must-see"
Whether for pleasure or as a duty!
I heard the constant clicking of Cameras
As we drove by the core and turn corners
People took photograph after photograph
For themselves and on others' behalf!
❖✧❖
◊

❖ ◇ ❖

◊

Oistins - 'Fish-fry' on a Friday night
Is truly a visitor's delight!
A meeting place for UK and USA visitors,
Returnees, family, brothers and Sisters;
Bumping into people you haven't seen for years;
❖ ◇ ❖
Seeing Hawkers flaunting their wares!
People mingling with their plate of Fish,
With Rice or Breadfruit, as they wish;
On sale also is yummy 'Fish-cake',
'Turnovers' and other sweet the Eatery make!

❖◇❖

Should you want an alternative way?
Check out **'Baxter's Road'** Fish bay
Where the aroma of fried fish fills the air,
Enticing one and all to draw near!

❖◇❖

Revisiting sometime in 1993,
Looking for refreshment near the sea;
Passing through the capital, Bridgetown
Would an ideal place be found?

❖◇❖

My relatives and I followed this trail
But nuisance caused our quest to fail;
We decided to settle for a 'Chefette' –
But the experience is hard to forget;
Don't know what happened on dat occasion?
As **Chefette** normally has a good reputation?

❖◇❖
◊

(Far from the days of home-cooked food –
The age of 'fast' and convenience I allude)!
Don't shoot me down, young people,
Times pass, some people's food had weevil!

❖◇❖

Many were brought up on 'Roast Breadfruit';

Few could this fact dispute?
Equally, Yams, Cassava and Eddoes,
Boiled or roasted sweet Potatoes!
❖◇❖
Freshly caught fish was commonly sold
To individuals and household!
You'll hear shouting - "Fish for sale
.... already boned and scaled"!
Hawkers carrying baskets do this
Or, Fishermen may sell their own fish!
One of them had to swallow a bitter pill
When his catch went sailing down Greggs Hill!
❖◇❖
◊

❖ ✦ ❖
◊

2013 was a delight for me in May;
A special treat, I'd say;
First-timers sister, niece and grandson
Experienced what it was like to be 'Bajan';
Easily embracing the lifestyle and culture,
Soaking up the 'sand, sea and sunny' weather;
Up early for the Island's round trip –
Nothing caused them this trip to skip!
Country roads provided jolts and a bumpy ride
But somehow, they took it all in their stride!
❖ ✦ ❖

❖✦❖

On-route to unforgettable **'River Bay'**
Stopping off at **'Farley Hill'** a visit pay;
Sighting Lakes; Belleplaine and **'East Coast'**;
'Bathsheba' and historic **St John** the last post!
Was the delicious food tops in all this?
Yes, **Oistin's** yummy fried fish!
Ask them – would they come again?
No prizes for guessing –
The Plane fare is part of the bargain!

❖✦❖

◊

Something I religiously have to do –
I believe it is the same for many of you?
Visiting notorious **'Swan Street'** –
Not for a stroll or something to eat,
But filling up with coconut water –
One of the items on my visit agenda!
There is where many make a 'bee-line';
Best period though, is mid-morning time!
No guarantee the stall will be there,
So hot-foot it to 'Independence Square'!
❖✧❖

I like topping up with water and jelly
And careful not to bust muh belly!
Swan Street is where you'll find visitors,
Returnees, sisters or brothers –
"Hey, I en no dat you hay"? (Here)
"I only call yuh name yesterday"!
(With sing-song talk, surprise and all),
You look around asking, "who made dat call"?

Is it human, **Flower** or mineral?
Fodder or a habitat for an **Animal**?
Someone please tell me bout dis **Cave**;
Is it a garden swept in by the waves?
Still don't know what's duh attraction!
Not because I haven't been often
Nor, is it for want of trying;
But, whenever I visit I end up sighing!
❖◇❖
Aged 10, I went there on a school trip;
Was told, "The cave is not viewing fit";
When revising the island, I tried again;
I couldn't believe I encountered the same!
Although disappointed, all was not lost,
I had to redeem the day at all cost!
So I explored the rugged rocks,
Forgetting about time or clocks;
Sat on the peak inhaling the fresh sea air;
Enjoying the privilege of being there!
❖◇❖
◊

CHAPTER 12

◊

HELP! BUGS IN PARADISE

❖◇❖

Even in Paradise, there's danger –
For locals and the intrepid stranger;
The mosquito sting that makes one squeal –
The cockroach that runs across your heel;

❖◇❖

Not forgetting the annoying sand flies,
So tiny, they're hard to see with naked eyes;
You'd try to pick up a tamarind seed –
Soon, out jump a wriggly millipede!

❖◇❖

Beware of the centipede and green lizard –
These two most people fear as hazard;
The peace of the tranquil night
Is broken by bats in flight!

❖◇❖

The darkness is illuminated by a 'fire-fly
The moment one comes whizzing by!
A peril I'm weary of, is the **mosquito attack**
Which, for me is a serious drawback!

❖◇❖

The mosquitoes had a sumptuous feast –
They came like Locusts out of the East;

Brothers and I were in the firing line
Especially at dusk and bedtime!
❖❖❖
Brother H was a pitiful sight -
He was covered with their harmful bite!
In an effort to keep us fairly secure,
We would close the wooden front door;
But, it was impossible to keep them out!
We thought of everything, even a water spout!
❖❖❖
Fearing their nasty sting cause us to break out in
sweat?
So we'd hang out by the beach to watch the sunset;
The West Coast became our temporary shelter,
But sooner we had to face the 'blood-suckers' after!
Caution! - To the foolish and wise;
There are bugs, even in Paradise!
❖❖❖
◊

CHAPTER 13

◊

SWEET PASTIMES / LIFE SKILLS - FOR REAL

❖◆❖

Residing near **Turner's Hall Woods**;

... Not sure whether this was for my good?

Yet, this provided a place to explore

Also help for many a chore!

❖◆❖

We had set daily chores;

Most times we'd pair in two's or four's!

But, frequently I had to travel alone

To sell Cashews in the next village or zone;

❖◆❖

Daring monkeys threatened me with their stare,

Causing my heart to pound with fear;

They would leap overhead from tree to tree

Indicating that they weren't scared of me!

❖◆❖

Being only aged ten,

(Helping family was usual for most children)!

Older folk demand respect;

We had to greet them whenever we met!

❖◆❖

They deem themselves a type of guardian

Who would scold you in love or fun!

No use you would to parents complain,
You'd be asking for more of the same!
❖◇❖
I'd say, a child at that time was no fool;
They certainly knew how to live by rule;
Not many were driven by an evil desire –
Afraid of scolding that would set their bum on fire!
Some did pranks and practiced awful schemes
But their cover was blown, by all means!
❖◇❖

In sunny weather or when the rain poured,
Cleaning the house was not ignored!
Other times, we'd play among the green marsh
Hidden out of sight as adults walk pass;
Gathering green or dry fire-wood -
Often catching our skin by sharp bramble!
❖◇❖
Fetching water from the standpipe
Where there would be a squabble or fight!
In crop season there was a water shortage,
So we fetch water from village to village;
At times from evening to next day at dawn,
Making us weary and forlorn!
However, Mammy would treat us to cake

Fresh from Miss Daisy's oven, baked!

◊

I loved Cray-fishing with uncle or brother;
Roasting our catch on the bank of the river!
Making dolls from ping-wing roots –
The slender tops of wild grass shoots;
Helping Auntie to wash baby's diaper
In the clear water at 'Back River'!
Detergent was mainly "OMO",
As people wanted their garments to glow!
A washing machine, many couldn't afford,
They resorted to the good old 'Jucking board'!
Then, there was the enduring 'Blue Soap'
Which removed stains - some did hope?
❖◇❖
Playing card games and others we invented
Some, very difficultly concocted!
Assisting at 'Bawden', pulling weeds -
Aiding the family's financial needs;
(Done only in the school holiday)
But, in groups, we found time to play!
❖◇❖
Carrying lunch for 'Pappy' on the farm,

To be back at school before the alarm!
Picking Cashews to sell in a nearby village;
A task, where I saw no privilege;
On account that I had to stay off school
Then, to be punished by the headmaster's tool!

❖◇❖

Nearby was our exciting playground;
Where our noises echoed in cheerily sound!
There, we had erected a swing
And kids showed off like eagles on wing!

❖◇❖

What makes children inquisitive?
That they have to check the negative
When you say, "don't touch",
Why are they aching to touch so much?

❖◇❖

This incident when 6 years old sprung to mind -
My ears were the hardest you could find;
There was something about 'Fish' I adore,
The melts and succulent 'Roe'!

❖◇❖

As small children we stood around the pot,
Waiting for the cooked Roe, although hot;
Was warned, "Don't touch the Roe on the plate";
But when backs were turned, I did the roe take!

❖◇❖

Soon, fits of horror and shame was mine
As my mouth was covered with fish slime;
I had taken the yarned Roe;
Oh... how my throat suffered, so?
The whole family were pulling and tugging
But I knew I was in for a flogging!
❖✧❖
◊

CHAPTER 14
◊

TASKING OUR BRAIN

A task we would give our memory
Is to identify any indigenous **tree**;

One which we easily call to mind
Is the mile tree which resembles the Pine;
The prickly Macaw and Spanish Oak;
Barcalocust and the Cabbage-coat
Where its skin was used as a skating boat!

❖◇❖

The Sandbox, Woman-tongue and Sycamore,
The Mahogany and the likeable Flambeau;
The fruitful Mango tree and Silk-cotton;
As its gawky shape is not easily forgotten!

❖◇❖

Some **fruits** too, are a task to remember –
But, our Orchard we could plunder!
We'd see Golden Apple, Cashew, and Guava;
Fat-pork, Plum, Pineapple, Mango;
Sour-sop; Paw-paw, Banana; (etcetera ...)

❖◇❖

In this wood is a myriad of trees,
Swinging from tree-tops are noisy monkeys;
I doubt you'll find any of them now;
They've left and gone to town, somehow!

❖◇❖
◊

Not too far from the broken down bridge,
Is the scenic plateau of 'the Ridge'
Where, floats the sweetest breeze,
A chosen spot of respite and serenity!

77

❖✧❖

'The woods' has some of the richest soil;
Shu..sh; I was told in the ground there's oil;
I believe it's called the 'Boiling Spring' -
Yet, not sure if any profit it did bring?

❖✧❖

Bubbles were seen coming out of the earth
It attracted tourists, for what it was worth;
Don't all run now with pick axe and spade -?
I doubt any millionaires were from it made!

❖✧❖
◊

CHAPTER 15
◊

POIGNANT MOMENTS
❖ ◊ ❖

Trying to find the family's gravestone
Which is often much overgrown
By thick weeds and long grass;
Finding it is a difficult task!
❖ ◊ ❖

Siblings and I go to pay mum our respect,
In an effort her, not to forget!
Even just walking through the graveyard
Where the soil is tardy and hard,
We'd head for the mahogany tree
Where the headstone was meant to be!
❖ ◊ ❖

(Respect also is due to our 'Granny'
Who, we lovingly called, 'Mammy';
She who was our dear guardian
When mum went to the United Kingdom!
Although we found her strict
She was fair and kept us healthy and fit!
A woman, godly to the core,
You had to do right, for sure!
❖ ◊ ❖

Prayers at Breakfast, Lunch and Supper –
Giving thanks for all things on offer!

If you were ever picked upon or blamed
She'd say, 'give up your right for wrong
Instead of causing a big ding dong'!
Or, 'just leave it up to God'
Who's the Giver of your reward"!
❖◇❖
Offspring were expected to read a verse
From the Bible they so often rehearsed;
When they were tucked up in bed to sleep
Without so much of a sound or a peep,
At midnight or break of day, she would say,
'Wakeup and pray; keep that old devil at bay'!
❖◇❖
Her home was always 'spick and span'
Although we could never understand
Why she should go to such extremes
But her standards had to be pristine!
To illustrate a lesson in tidiness
That, 'cleanliness was next to godliness'!
❖◇❖
Her doors were open to all alike
For shelter, comfort and refreshing delights;
Whatever the time of day no one could say,
'I left her house without a word of prayer'!
Her good morals were never in question

When she faced an intricate decision!
❖◇❖
If you were feeling lone or sad
Because of some problems you've had
And fears and burdens weighed you down
Until your sorrows you could drown,
These words of wisdom she would share –
"God don't put on us more than we could bear"!
❖◇❖
She was a woman of prudence and etiquette,
Who believed music is Heaven's best gift, yet;
Urging you to make music or sing a song,
On chilly nights when the hours seem long;
She encouraged good attention to health,
Saying, "get a book and educate yourself"!)
❖◇❖
◊

After Mammy's death we had times of leanness;
This, I reluctantly confess
When, three children fall prey to hunger;
Bellies grumbling, they huddled together!
❖◇❖
The result of was one sad and mournful day
One we'd like to forget, you might say;
Life gave us a foul surprise;

By sad news that came in disguise -
We were told, "You must leave school now,
Your 'Mammy' is ailing, somehow"!
❖◆❖
By the time we got to see her face,
Her spirit had gone to another place?
Were we now left for ourselves to fend?
Who would take care of the children?
Would the news get to the parents abroad?
❖◆❖
Questions, turmoil and upheaval;
Hardship and misery seemed inevitable
But, we kept Mammy's good principle -
'Love each other'; 'give' and 'share';
This helped us to alleviate some of our care!
❖◆❖
Time pass and some of us went to the UK
To continue our education and work there!
However, not forgetting our roots,
Always yearning for life's first fruits!
❖◆❖
(We must now leave the grave yard -
Reluctantly, whether it's easy or hard;
And let the ancestors have their rest;
They've enough in our lives invest!
❖◆❖

◊

CHAPTER 16
◊

RE-TRACING OUR STEPS- THE OLD PATH
❖ ❖ ❖

As we return time and again,
The parish life seemed the same!
We'd head for 'Nan-yan Gap', the back-drop
From our old house spot!
Always featured in our plans to explore
Although tricky to find, for sure!
❖ ❖ ❖
We'd create a path through the overgrowth,
Using sticks or cutlass or both;
Chatter of pranks we did as children,
Laughing loudly, retelling them!
❖ ❖ ❖
Uphill, we slipped and slide in the bracken
As the rain had recently fallen
Yet, it was a joy to reach the hilly breeze,
To climb and sit in the whistling trees!
Sighting Mount Hillaby's breathtaking view,
Overlooking White Hill and Chalky-mount too!
❖ ❖ ❖
We found the place we played 'hopscotch' –
For hours and hours, not wanting to stop!

Tried to identify the neighbours' landmarks –
A quest, not knowing where to start!
Naming them and their characteristics -
Only those of substance, albeit!
❖◇❖
In an effort to preserve treasured memory
That all who passes by may see –
The initial D; H; O and name, Ruby
I etched on the spiky 'Silk-grass'
So that forever these could last!
❖◇❖
A firm confession, I would not lie;
One belonging to my siblings and I
That, the East Coast is our firm favourite,
So we head there every time we visit!
❖◇❖
One night we stayed there by the beach;
Near to 'Lakes', within easy reach;
Pleasuring the sea air we found,
Sitting among the grape vines on the ground;
Watching the swirling waves break,
Enjoying the therapeutic noise they'd make;
Our minds took a trip down memory lane,
Whether it provided loss or gain?
Wrapped in the historical moment,

But soon it was jolted back to the present -
We didn't want to miss the last bus to Bridgetown
For to walk over 40 miles was too long!

◊

CHAPTER 17

◊

MILES FROM BRIDGETOWN

❖◇❖

❖◇❖

Is the mini-van a must for all to use?
Is it a necessity? You choose!
This comment I've heard say
By folk because of travel-fear;
"Riding to Bridgetown by mini-van
Is a novelty that should be banned"?
Some drive at an illegal speed
While passengers cry for mercy, plead!
The music blaze out ridiculously loud,
Yet, it pleases the youthful crowd!
❖ ◇ ❖
◊

Do you fancy walking from '**Bridgetown**'?
All the way to your home-ground?
Trust me; this has already been done;
You ask; did this person carry a gun?
By all means, there's Lorton pick-up van
But, you'd have to rustle for a seat if you can?
❖ ◇ ❖
Here are places you'd pass along the way;
I cannot tell how you would fair?
Careful not to step on 'Crapo' or Centipede,
'Hard-back worms' or 'Millipede'!
❖ ◇ ❖
By foot you head towards '**Eagle Hall**'
Still walking, you give 'Green Hill' a call;
No stopping for shopping at '**Warren**',

Not even for a 'nit bottle' of Gin!
Turn towards **'Jacksons'** and **'Edge Hill'**
Up the steepness of classy 'Shop Hill'!
❖ ◆ ❖

You could rest a little as you choose
As you approach the village of **'Vaucluse'**;
Whether you know 'Content' or not
At this place you should not stop!
Don't know why it is so called
But don't linger to discover it at all!
❖ ◆ ❖

Turn and go around **'Barker's Corner'** -
No stopping with friends or farmer;
You still have a long way to go -
That you should surely know!
❖ ◆ ❖

Set your sights for **'Porey Spring'**;
Never mind its tranquillity or anything!
Keep going till you approach **'Dunscombe'**;
Here, soon **'Farmers'** will beckon!
You've done about half your journey'
Just keep focus and you'll see!
Turn the corner; down to **'Farm part'**;
Careful of the sharp bend; take heart!
❖ ◆ ❖

Next landmark is **'Bottom Hope'** -
Rest for a drink of 'Juicy' or 'Coke'! (Cola)
'Top Hope' is just up the hill;
Turn left there but don't stand still!

You're now in the village of 'Hillaby' –
No charge for its scenic view, it's all free!
❖◇❖

Down to 'Moose Bottom'; up 'Greggs Hill' –
There's about 3 miles to go, still!
Enter the quaint hamlet of 'Turners Hall';
Be ready to walk through its woods and all!
❖◇❖

Unfortunately, there're no signposts,
So you'll have to rely on instincts or ghosts;
(Talk says, some were in these parts,
Claiming, they have even left their mark)!
❖◇❖

Now, turn right by the 'Silk Cotton Tree',
Via 'Highland Hill' where a bridge will be!
Keep straight until you get to 'Top Gap'
Without turning, 'though you may spot a rat!
'Nan-yan Gap' is right up ahead;
Don't turn in, just have a break instead!
❖◇❖

Next, is the slope of 'Pond Bottom'
A short distance from 'Shoulder Mutton'!
(Don't look for water or a Pond -
All aspects of these are now gone)!
❖◇❖

Afterwards, is the awful 'Break-away',
Indicating your journey's end is near!
You breathe a sigh of relief –
There's life in sight, 'good-grief'!

Enter **St Simons**, your desired goal;
Pat yourself on the back for being so bold!
❖✧❖
◊

CHAPTER 18

◊

'BAJAN LINGO', OLD SAYINGS AND PROVERBS

❖ ❖ ❖

From birth **Lingo** was part of you;
Expressing it in words rich and true
Yet, you're told to speak the Queen's English,
Where in your house you were admonished!

❖ ❖ ❖

Wah yuh sey?
(What did you say?)

❖ ❖ ❖

Don't pelt me with nuff big rocks
If I uncover any of yuh old pocks;
Just trying to mek yuh lafh
I don't on yuh any stone cast!

❖ ❖ ❖

Yuh sey she wid dat hardairs hole?
She jus donh wanna be told;
Not 'cause she weak,
She just got a stubborn streak;
But I guine lick it outta she,
Cos she belong tuh me!

❖ ❖ ❖

Wah yuh bein suh malicious fuh?,

Dah fuh lick yuh!
Yuh tink I born yestaday?
If yuh touch me, yuh guine pay;
Move yuh self from buhfor muh!

❖ ◇ ❖

I saw yuh boy skinning cuffin wid he friend;
Like dey got de devil in dem!
Yuh can't find nuh employment fuh he?
Give im a Hoe or keep im under lock and key!

❖ ◇ ❖
◊

SOME INTERPRETATION OF BAJAN 'LINGO'

Bim - Barbados
Dan - than
Dat - that
Dem - them
Dese - these
Dey - they
Duh; - the
Fuh - for
Guh - go
Hay - here
Leh - let

Muh - my
Mo - more
Nuh - no
Nutten - nothing
'O' - of
Pon - upon/on
Suh - so
Sey - see
Trute - truth
Wid - with
Wha - what
Yuh - you

◊

PROVERBS

◊

I often heard my grand-parents with the following proverbs; perhaps, some were of their own making:

"Yuh never miss de water till de well run dry"!

"Cleanliness is next to godliness"!

"When monkey got money, he does buy nuts"!

"Necessity is the mother of invention"!

"A stitch in time saves nine"!

"Never wash yuh dirty linen in public"!

CHAPTER 19

◊

SWEET SCHOOL DAYS

❖ ✧ ❖

❖ ✧ ❖

My school days came flooding back -
St Simons' School had now become a shack
Unfortunately, losing every nail and tact!
But for old times' sake, I its steps climbed,
Ignoring the broken windows and blinds;
Satisfying myself, so it seems
I walked across broken, dilapidated beams!

❖ ✧ ❖

An airy feeling of nostalgic bliss
Mixed with anguish my mind kissed;
Recalling the Head's strap of punishment,
For lateness or merely his resentment!
Remembering games I played with friends,
When things went wrong and made amends?
❖◇❖
Accolades given for being top of the class,
In certain subjects or difficult tasks;
Of milk and biscuits as we stood in line,
In the morning period and break-time!
❖◇❖
I smuggled my 3 year old brother into school
Despite this being against the rule -
Hiding him under my cramped desk,
So his presence no one might guess;
My cover was blown near the end of the day,
So he was graciously allowed to stay!
❖◇❖
Primary School days for me were sweet;
Favourite subject, History was a treat;
Studying bout Alfred the Great and such like,
Their heroic battles and bitter fight;
Getting lost in the Inca and Aztec civilisation
Using every bit of my imagination!

Music Class was also a joy
When with songs my voice I'd employ;
In class competition I'll be second or first,
Whether the songs were new or previously rehearsed
I'm not at all ashamed to say
That I actually cried on my last school day!

❖ ◇ ❖
◊

Sir Conward Hunte taught me in Class A;
When, **to Cricket**, he was called away!
He was teaching me to write that day
As I stood upon a little chair;
Being only five years old then,
I was truly heart-broken!
This is not a claim to fame, I must add
Just the event made me so sad!
Passing through familiar Belleplane,
Thoughts of it filled my mind again;
❖ ◇ ❖
Sat the 11-plus, called the 'Screening Test;
Came first in my school; I surely did my best?
(Not boasting that I was brilliant,
I deem myself an average student
And acknowledge the sweet favour
From a loving Heavenly Father)!
❖ ◇ ❖
◊

97

HIGH SCHOOL

❖◇❖

Going on to further education,
It was the 'Alleyne', a nearby location –
"Allis non Sibi" - For others, not ourselves!
Pupils practiced this and in it delve!
I'd say, an admirable fitting Motto,
By Sir John Gay Alleyne, its Founder!
❖◇❖
A former pupil - it gives me much delight
A poem in its honour, write;
Although spending three years there,
I'm thrilled some stories to share!
With this poem I the school commemorate
And my time there, appreciate!
❖◇❖
In it lay many secret joys and sorrow;
Lessons learnt from which we could borrow!

An ominous trip down memory lane
May cause some to quiver, all the same -
Fearful of the Headmaster's cane!
For others, a time of pleasure and fun,
Playing games with friends under the hot sun!
❖◇❖
Many anticipating an eventful 'Speech Day'
Or fighting back graduation fear?
Some held a cricket ball and bat
Scoring good runs or a brilliant catch!
However we recall, it's a sure fact
That the Alleyne is a 'shining Star' on the map!
❖◇❖
Many people of talent from it have emerged,
Making a difference in their world to serve;
Plenty emigrated to Canada and the USA
Whilst countless others settled in the UK
They, congregating at the Alumni events
Providing input and conveying compliments!
❖◇❖
Forgetting demographics and all,
We'll not try to do a roll call
Since, we've lost many friends along the way
And their absence for some is hard to bear;
But their purposes have been fulfilled,

Leaving behind their footprints, still!
Yet, in bitter-sweet reflection
We'll give a toast to them on this occasion!
❖ ❖ ❖
Pupils came from Belleplaine and all around,
Perhaps, as far afield as Bridgetown!
In reflecting - on the way to Belleplaine
We'd pass by Walkers' field of cane;
❖ ❖ ❖
If driving via windy Farley Hill,
We'd look over the East Coast for a scenic fill!
Most relied on their feet for transport
And in droves along winding roads they'd float;
Sounds of boys and girls chatting together
About school lessons or any other matter!
❖ ❖ ❖
A treat for some were wine berries
When they pass by John Cox's territory!
Pupils emerged from White Hill and Hillaby,
St. Simons, Haggats Hill and the Shorey;
Cane Garden, Triapath and Bruce vale;
Some on bicycles or maybe, a lift they'll hail!
Others coming from idyllic Lakes
May walk with Salt-bread and Fish Cakes?
Oops! Did I really say that?

Out of the bag, I've let the cat!
... Dreaming of Fish-Cakes from Mrs Moore –
The ones we did truly adore!

❖◇❖

The Smith's family too, where we'd go first
For ice-cold drinks to quench our thirst!
These people truly deserve a mention
And yes, this calls for a Celebration!
Somehow, a special time was **the 60's era**,
Don't all shout now, maybe later!

❖◇❖

Turning the spotlight on teachers like, Mr Gay,
I wonder what each pupil would have to say?
Here's someone else you may remember -
A former pupil who returned as a teacher;
The shapely Ms Richardene Clark;
You'd rely on her to give you a fair mark!

❖◇❖

Others, who returned and taught as well,
Were Mr Jordan and Mr Campbell!
Another, was the enduring Mr Doughlin
Who mastered the translation of Latin!
The person we'd not dare to match
Is the Headmaster, Mr D C Cumberbatch!
I hesitate..., no more names I'll call

As a story might leak out, interestingly tall?

❖◇❖

Again, we honour **Sir John Gay Alleyne**
For the good his legacy bearing;
May we all with mutual respect,
Embrace his most worthy concept;
Place hands on heart and agree,
With cheerful shouts – '**Allis Non Sibi**'!

❖◇❖
◊

Attending school, there was no school bus
So walking all the way was a must;
However, this provided joyful fruits,
As, we mainly travel in groups
Merrily chatting about life and home work
Which, often alone you'll have to research!
Togetherness provided a safety net,
Allaying parent's anxiety, yet!

❖◇❖

There weren't many cars in our district;
Not as if you could choose one or pick,
Yet, a certain man offered us a lift
Even though we may resist!

❖◇❖

If we should spot him in the distance,

Hiding away would be our preference;
We'd run and hide amongst the sugar cane;
Just the dust from our feet would remain!
We didn't want to be seen in a decrepit car
Although the journey to school was quite far!
❖◇❖

At times pupils would travel alone;
Not everyone had access to a telephone
To arrange meeting up with friends,
At a place where your parent recommends?
❖◇❖

Once, I was on my way home;
Travelling from school on my own
When the local Postman like a bird in flight
Came by riding on his motor-bike;
❖◇❖

He offered me a ride from Belleplaine;
I quickly accepted, all the same;
Not sure whether I was thrilled or fearful
But I held on him tightly and compliable?
❖◇❖

He soon took off with great speed;
The wind pushing us along, indeed!
Just as he turn up steep 'Haggetts Hill,
I jumped off the bike, at will!
❖◇❖

I had never rode on a bike before
So I thought we might crash, for sure!
Heavens helped – I landed on my feet
Without having medical help to seek!
Thankfully, I had not a broken bone;
Just a dent in my confidence was shown!
When I got home I kept this to myself;
I didn't want a bitter pill from off duh shelf!

Vacation time was a tasteful pleasure
For indulging in fun and intrepid adventure!
Last day of term we'd burst into song
At the expectant peal of the Gong –
"No more Latin, no more French;
No more sitting on de old hard bench"!
Yet, Mammy insisted on Saturday sessions
Of some tedious private lessons!

CHAPTER 20

◊

SIBLINGS' TEASING/GOLDEN DAYS

❖❖❖

Travelling through the pitch dark woods;
When a smut lamp did great good
As the only source of light
When we huddled together for fright;
No one wanted to be at the back -,
This being difficult, as a matter of fact!
Siblings said, I was scared of my shadow
Yet, acted like a sir-warrior and terror!
Mind you, one of us didn't do many tasks –
This question I would ask;
Who then got off scotch-free?
I wonder who this person might be.

❖❖❖

Someone would rub their eyes and plead
Whenever it was their turn to **read**;
Yet, when promised a piece of sweet bread,
You'd hear eloquence in what this person said;
This ploy was not deem to last
As Mammy found out; it was only a farce!
No! Oh no! Stop thinking it was me,
The clue is my sibling - name ending 'ley'!

❖❖❖

'Special' are our childhood years
When we shared much joy and tears
With care and great understanding
That binds us with heartfelt meaning!
Oceans separated us from our parents,
We'd offer each other encouragement!
❖◇❖
Who straightened the boys' hair with a fork?
Not fearing what Mammy thought;
Was it cousin X who was to blame?
Don't want to tarnish my good name!
Why were we often scold? - One plus three;
Two brothers, a cousin and me;
Were we that mischievous?
Or, just daringly adventurous?
Perhaps, there was an instigator;
Ha, ha,... I'll not now be a traitor!
❖◇❖
Who invented the game called 'Potta'
That we played in the Veranda?
Executed with bottle-tops
Of 'Juicy' - sweet fizzy pops;
Chalk-drawn white squares
Held our attention many years!
❖◇❖

Not to mention 'picks-up' and 'Jacks',
'Hopscotch' – producing acrobats!
'Rummy' and numerous 'go-to-pack,
Formed part of the act!
Broken plates, shaped round,
Provided another game we found;
Along with 'tamarind' seeds,
Gathered amongst the weeds!
Good we could laugh about all this,
Those were **'Golden days'**, I insist!
❖ ◆ ❖
Often, we'd indulge in sweet reflection
Of by-gone days of marked perception
When desires were not met,
Still, we embrace no blame or regret;
Like, the time we longed for a Xmas tree
And to see Father Xmas – could this be?
We wished uncle could fulfil our expectation
And bring the dream into fruition;
However, he'd secretly fled in the night
To the UK, he had taken a flight!
Yet, I deem the trials **countless treasure**,
Un-exchangeable and intact forever!
But lessons of life compel us to learn -
'Live for today and tomorrow, give no concern'!

CHAPTER 21

◊

BIGGING UP ST ANDREW

❖◇❖

Nuff said? No! I must big-up **St Andrew**;
Not just for the idyllic East Coast and view;
Although small and countrified
Countless graces it did provide!
Not to mention those who sought repose,
That came in their hundreds to its shores!

❖◇❖

Born in this place were people of renown
With various talents, professionally sound!
Some who made a significant impact
To the island's economy where it lacked:
Those who immigrated to another country
Contributed greatly to their community!

❖◇❖

In Sports and also in the Arts
Each one playing their positive parts;
Contributing still in a place like the UK,
Parts of Canada and the USA -
In public Transport and the Health Service
Generally and when there's a crisis!
Some may know those to whom I refer

And this mention may your memory stir?

❖ ✦ ❖

◊

Many may remember Sir Conrad Hunte
Whose honour I want to push up-front;
He was my primary school teacher
Before he excelled as a Cricketer!
Born in Shorey Village Plantation,
He was an outstanding Cricket Batsman;
(Also a former 'Alleynian)!
He played for the West Indies in the 1950's and 60's
Where he scored runs over eight centuries!
In fact, it's on record as 3,245;
One of the best scores of batsmen dead or alive!
He was conferred the **highest honour** in Barbados,
Being made a "Knight of St Andrew" – Yes! Yes!

❖ ◇ ❖
◊

Folks, **St Andrew** have done it again!
This Parish will never remain the same?
Remember cricketing legend, John Shepherd,
Another Alleynian, I hasten to add;
He's inducted in the US Cricket **Hall of Fame'**
So, please remember his name!
In his debut he took 5 wickets as fast bowler
Against England in Manchester!
His career extended over two decades
Where in far flung places he played;
Like England, West Indies and Rhodesia!
If his many feats you've not heard about
With elation you're now free to shout!
❖ ◇ ❖
Others also deserve a mention for sure
But these two, I've met before!
Yet, many embarked on careers
As Dentists, Doctors, and Engineers;
Nurses, Midwives and Teachers;
Business professionals and Lawyers!
This goes to genuinely show
That the younger generation should know
That there's room at the top to spare

111

And you can get there from anywhere!
❖✧❖
I must give **St Andrew** a hearty applause,
Asking 'Andrew-ites' to join me in this cause;
Don't be shy or, think it's hard work;
No need your duty to shirk;
Let's bring out the appealing 'Steel Band'
And dance to the rhythm so grand!
You oldies could tap yuh feet
While duh young ones could jump and leap!
❖✧❖
◊

CHAPTER 22
◊

BAJAN CROP-OVER
❖◇❖

Is it duh end of the Sugar Cane Harvest
When Bajans celebrate with euphoria and zest?
When planeloads of people come from all bout
To jump, work-up and shout?
❖◇❖
You want me tuh mention Kadooment?
Can't say much boh; betta ask dem who went!
I visited 'Bim' a couple times at 'Crop-over'
Due tuh duh sickness of muh mother!
❖◇❖

I went tuh a calypso tent one night;
Yes, I tink dats right!
What year was dat and muh age?
Well, I tink 'Macfingal' was on stage?

❖◇❖

Duh Bank Holiday I started for 'Spring Garden'
But, decided it was too hot to be marching!
I opted for stirring "Breadfruit Cuckoo"
And plenty of King Fish on duh top, too!"
I did steam some, I did fry some
But, I din lef yuh none!

❖◇❖

Mind yuh, duh music was sweet, too sweet,
So **'Inez'** had to turn off she potta meat!
Some man tell Inez to **"come down"** –
Don't know if she made it to town?
But duh music was sweet, still too sweet;
Yuh had tuh dance duh 'Crop-over' beat!
Yuh kno someting? Afta all dese years,
Dat tune still ringing in muh ears!

❖◇❖

Another Calypsonian I heard doing a gag
Was the infamous **'Red Plastic Bag'**!
A Lotta yuh might know his songs
And what year each one belongs!

❖◇❖

Dis tune I heard, very much aired
Was 'Obadiah'; on the radio frequently played!
I believe it successfully won a contest
Being voted the 'Crop-over' season's best!
Dats all I got fuh yuh;
I can't do nuh more fuh yuh!
❖◇❖
◊

CHAPTER 23

M2/FOOT WORK FOR TRANSPORT

❖ ❖ ❖

Should you fancy taking the scenic view?
You could resort to M2 (my two)!
Walking everywhere on foot
Could be a danger, even encountering a crook
Lurking in the dense woods or Sugar canes
To pounce on lonesome travellers, in the main!
One said, they saw a crook on their way
But persuaded him a godly life, sway!

❖ ❖ ❖

I loved the days when about four or six;
(Those events in my head still stick),
Times I travel with family on a Sunday morning;
Waking before cock-crowing!
On foot from St Andrew to Spaw Hill,
Bracing the sweet air cool or chill;
Mind you, it was a happy experience, still!
Daddy was an itinerant Preacher;
Me, a doting Minister's daughter!

❖ ❖ ❖

Travelling from Parish to Parish on foot
Bracing it for as long as it took!
Some places we visited quite a lot
Like, 'Chimborazo' and breezy 'Airy cot'!

Less seldom was 'Mile and Quarter'
And a place in St John called, 'Venture'!
❖◇❖
Other times, walking was bitter-sweet;
Through rough places with sore feet;
Going with family for the weekly provision -
To St Thomas, was my decision!
For this trip we'd seek short-cuts
Through gullies, cane fields and such!
Arousing several dogs was a drawback;
Being vulnerable to their attack;
Plantation dogs chased us as they loudly bark;
As you may guess, they were viciously sharp!
❖◇❖
Dogs were not muzzled but on the loose,
Allowed to run wild, their ego to boost!
They'd sense your presence a long distance away
And run to attack you because them you fear!
❖◇❖
Once, carrying dinner for great-grandfather,
I was chased by the dog of a neighbour;
The bowl of food went flying in the air;
No one was in sight for me to care;
I swiftly ran, hitting my head to a tree,
Knocking me out and making me dizzy!
❖◇❖
Could it be that the dog smelt the food?
Or were they in a foul mood?
I was the victim whatever the reason,

Left without redress or compensation!
❖◇❖
Glad to say, bad things have an end;
It's not if, but when?
Not long after, someone else they had bitten
Causing their action to be in question;
The owners had to face the law court
On account of the victim's report!
❖◇❖
I was glad when I moved to another area
Where dog owners were responsibly fairer!
Yet, fate would have its ploy
That, instead of dogs I had to fend off boys;
Being 'the new girl in town',
A group of them followed me around;
I intending to keep myself pure,
But they tried hard, me to know!
❖◇❖
Once, they formed a line across my path
Determined a human net to cast;
Blocking my way so I couldn't pass!
"Heavens help! This is ten persons to one;
Had to think fast – this isn't fun";
So in courageous confidence I started to run!
Like... running through a troop; leaping over a wall;
Keeping head above the water; standing tall!
Never again did boys block my way;
As fate would have it, I escaped to the UK!

CHAPTER 24

◊

STILL SUCKING SUGAR-CANE

❖✧❖

The highlight of my 68th year –
Yes, some month to my birthday,
I joyfully chewed and sucked sugar-cane
Giving thanks for the opportunity again
To lay into the sweet, juicy cane!
A blessing, I hasten to add,
As some others watching, appear sad!
They couldn't enjoy this delightful treat;
Having been robbed of their teet! (Teeth)

❖◇❖

This pastime seemed not so far away
When, as a child I sucked cane many a day;
In the crop season with my family
Preparing bundles of cane for the factory!
(Many of them were in good operation
But now, most are abandoned)!

❖◇❖

Youngsters knew how to live by rule -
Embracing **ambition** as their tool!
There was no practice of idleness –
More like, when do we get to rest?
Glad that cane is found in the UK now
Although it's not the same, somehow!
'The real McCoy' is my delight –
Sucking sugar cane on a moonlit night!
I'd rather go to 'Bim' for the true taste
To enjoy reflective moments without haste,
When dreams would awaken my childhood era
That's wrapped in unforgettable pleasure!

❖◇❖
◊

9 780995 683709